*She reconsiders
life on the run*

Tricia Dearborn

She reconsiders life on the run

IPSI CHAPBOOK 2.2

University of Canberra
International Poetry Studies Institute
Series editor: Paul Munden

UNIVERSITY OF CANBERRA

International Poetry Studies Institute
Faculty of Arts and Design
University of Canberra
Canberra, Australia
http://ipsi.org.au

Poems © Tricia Dearborn 2019
Design: Caren Florance

ISBN 978-0-6485537-6-2

Contents

The white dress	1
A chalk outline of the soul	2
The smiley spoon	3
Sanctuary	4
She reconsiders life on the run	6
The changes	8
Come in, lie down	9
Phlegm: a love poem	10
The quiet house	13
Nessa	16
Vita	17
Ethel	18
The pouch of Douglas	19
Making pipettes	20
[50] Tin	21
[82] Lead	22
[20] Calcium	23
[11] Sodium	24
Scar massage	26
Everything including the obvious	28
Notes	31
Acknowledgements	32
Biography	34

The white dress

I knelt with your sewing scissors
beside the towering wardrobe

carefully I snipped holes in
your authority

I would see my life
through those holes

creating them I rained to the red rug
triangles of fine white corduroy

I would not wear that dress

A chalk outline of the soul

Sister Pascal sketched on the blackboard
a human soul
her impromptu rendition –
which I believed anatomically exact –
shaped like a vertical dog's bone
but wider at the bottom and more angular.

She dotted it with chalk
which was original sin
then removed each smutch with the duster
which was God's grace
as manifested in baptism, marriage –
in all the seven sacraments.

That was the year I learnt
how you made words with letters,
imbibed the way their patterns
created sound and meaning, divined
that in spite of this some words
conformed to no rule but their own.

While Sister Pascal taught God's grace –
the one route to redemption –
as chrism, wedding band,
Eucharist, a small white moon
on a silver salver,
quietly I married the word.

The smiley spoon

The wooden spoon regarded rage or tears
with a drawn-on frown
before being turned to show the smile
that we must match, or feel its bite.

We killed it once. A dawn raid
on the second drawer. Snapped it
clean in two. Next day its twin appeared.

In her childhood kitchen, my first love
had dodged the stinging blows
of a kettle cord.

She learnt how to mete out bruises.
I learnt how to smile like a spoon.

Sanctuary

We woke to that kitchen's
good morning smell of toast

its squares of lino,
green, blue and red

that we hopscotched across,
the gas stove that leaked a little

so that, to this day, a faint smell of gas
is homey and slightly magical.

Played in the long backyard
with the old cracked path,

its lemon tree, dahlias, frangipani,
beans and mandarins, passionfruit vine.

Or in Grandpa's stone-floored garage,
always cool, with its thick dark

smell of engine oil. At night
we lay wakeful in the small wooden beds

with the built-in drawers
or on the mattress laid between them

claiming each train in turn,
each of us wanting the last of the night

to be ours, the winner announced
by a lengthening peace.

From the small recessed window
the Virgin Mary in her blue robes

watched over us, arms outstretched.
The bathroom had a noisy glass towel rail,

a high old-fashioned light switch
still out of my reach at seven.

In the sheltering night of that house
when I called out to Mum

she'd come to me
from the back verandah.

In the hallway, the child Christ clings
to a knowing-eyed Madonna.

He's run to her from his bed,
one sandal dangling.

The angels to either side
with their terrifying portents.

She reconsiders life on the run

Sadness always knew where to find me, though I kept on giving it false addresses, and moved house when it got too close. It discovered my silent number. Tired of its voice on the answering machine, I disconnected the phone.

I took to leaving the lights off so sadness couldn't tell when I was at home. I didn't put music on. I moved around as little as possible in case it had sonar. I wasn't sure how it was tracking me.

It got so that it was hard to go out. I'd be standing in the supermarket choosing a brand of shampoo and sadness would touch my elbow. I'd realise in the cinema as the lights went down that sadness had the seat next to me.

Eventually I saved up and had my fingerprints removed and my face reconstructed by a plastic surgeon so sadness wouldn't recognise me, even if we bumped into each other on the street.

The day sadness saw me and knew me in my new face and hands I realised it was going to take a heart transplant to shake this thing. The excitement of living like a get-away driver was beginning to pall.

I decided to reclaim my face, my actual address. I know that sadness will choose inconvenient times to visit, arriving as I'm getting dressed to go out, or at 2am, or while I'm watching my favourite show on TV.

But it doesn't unpack its suitcase all over my bedroom, or drink all the milk, or run up a three-figure phone bill calling long-distance, or expect to stay for months like an English backpacker.

And now I don't have to avert my gaze when sadness catches my eye, or block my ears when it knocks at the door. Now I say, Is it you, sadness? Come in, come in, it's been a while.

The changes

Kissing Louise was a bell. Unlike
the chimes of the genteel drawing-room clock
it gave no warning before it struck.

It was more like the shock of the extra-early
morning alarm
on the day of the journey.

Or the sudden shrilling of a schoolroom bell,
calling me in
to a strange new lesson.

It rang sweet as a tardy dinner gong
summoning me to a meal
of scent and heat.

Resonated like a great church bell
calling the villagers over fields
to christenings, to benedictions.

My throat sang my body
swung my skin shone
and my old life shivered and fell from me

and lay like the sweat of the ringers in the tower.

Come in, lie down

I'm new to you and your let's-get-to-it.
Flat on my back that first time
not five minutes after the front door

snicked behind you. New to this
excoriating tenderness, passion
that leaves me stubble-scraped and scabbed.

The shock of those minuscule nipples!
The lean hairy thigh that met my palm
and made me laugh out loud. Later you asked

was it OK, for sex with an alien?
Women are sea-creatures, you said,
one hand curved at the soft swell of my thigh.

Like seals. And men are goats. I like you
inside me, when I want it. I like how you held my hair back
that first time we stood there kissing. You come

so close to sating me with touch, stroke into me
relaxation I rarely know;
round up and banish ancient threats

whose names I'm beginning not to recognise. Still –
I miss that brine-lapped cleft, the way that sealskin
glides on sealskin. One day I must

go down to the seas again.

Phlegm: a love poem

I'm reading Maggie Nelson
occasionally stopping to cough up phlegm
in some indeterminate post-fever stage of the flu

she's living on a canal with a junkie boyfriend
or that's how I read it

the poems might as well be called 'no good will come of it'
raging despair oozes out of them
toxic as the canal's stinking sludge
or my almost fluorescent yellow-green phlegm

I hack
'Spit,' says my mind
I spit out on the tissue
'Good girl,' I say out loud

I learnt this

my mother, not big on emotion or touch,
excelled at sickbed ritual

earlier tonight I was telling my girlfriend
(scavenger of sleep, getting what she can between my bouts)
how it calmed me as a child, calms me now

the bucket by the bed in case you were sick
the towel laid cross-wise on the bed underneath you
in case you didn't quite get to the bucket
its strange comforting roughness
the smell of disinfectant
when the bucket came back fresh

then I instructed her in percussive therapy
another thing I learnt from my mother
it breaks up the phlegm

she pounded me on the back as I lay angled off the sofa
head resting on my forearms on the ground
up/down from the waist to the top of the shoulder blades

then helped me back onto the sofa
where I lay sweating
while she looked on with patient palpable concern

I notice we get on better when I'm sick
she less defensive and kinder
I more vulnerable, less autocratic

at night a Buteyko technique I found on the internet
eases the coughing
to begin, you take a breath
and hold it 'till discomfort'
the aim is to create *air hunger*

lately I'm learning to tolerate
the right kinds of discomfort
to honour the hungers my mother discounted

Maggie tells her boyfriend
it's not the content / I'm in love with, it's the form

how can you separate
a slender torso, small breasts, their exuberant nipples
a clitoris that is a chameleon to the tongue
now rampant, now indiscernible
somehow melded back into bone
from the love, the rightness
the great goodwill

her habits with time which are mine with money
no planning
then blaming the shortfall
on some unexpected but perfectly foreseeable circumstance

her face turned to me on the sofa
its energy and joy
dark circles under her eyes
because I've been keeping her up at night
coughing

The quiet house

i.m. Scarlett Vallence, 7 September 2008

i. Family portrait

At the top of the photograph,
J's face. Grief pours off him

like a glacier, monumental.
My eyes move down to you,

your gaze on the child
who lies across your ribs.

Your face a wall. Behind it
the gathering tsunami.

ii. Nightmare

on the drugs that are meant
to help you sleep,
you dream –

a camera pans along a row
of fat pink wriggling infants
the line is long, the camera

moves swiftly
you struggle desperately to wake –
you know your small still baby's

last in line

iii. Small comfort

At the wake, champagne in hand,
J and I amuse ourselves inventing
more offensive ways of swearing –

J's brother poses our family photo,
tousling your hair and mine,
dragging our brothers' ties askew –

I'm handed a cigarette, inhale
the small comfort of an old habit.
It ends

when J sobs in our arms
then struggles free. Your urgent whisper:
What do you want? What do you want?

iv. The quiet house

I sit in the cool leather chair
in your back room

looking out to the morning garden
with my cup of tea.

Such peace – when what I want
is her, here

squalling against my chest
while you have a grateful shower.

v. Ashes

My suitcases
stand in the hall.

I hesitate, but when I
finally ask

you say *Of course*.
I bend to lift her

from the cot.
Gently

I rock her, pat
the quilt-wrapped box.

Nessa

'I always feel I'm writing more for you than for anybody.'
—*Virginia Woolf, letter to Vanessa Bell, 15 October 1931*

From the moment of that chance encounter
under the nursery table

when she asked you if black cats had tails
and you said no

she was your co-conspirator,
your best-beloved

rival – painter to your writer,
fruitful to your childless,

stoic to your voluble,
Dolphin to the Billy Goat

and later – you were often plural
in your affections – to the Apes

who hooted and wooed her.
You considered yourself her firstborn.

Demanded your 'rights' –
those kisses and pettings.

Without her you merely existed,
dry and dusty.

With her,
you would always be the child

who fingered her amethyst necklace,
naming with each bead

a person she loved,
a jealousy.

Vita

'... she shines in the grocer's shop in Sevenoaks with a candle lit radiance, stalking on legs like beech trees, pink glowing, grape clustered, pearl hung.'
—*Virginia Woolf, diary, 21 December 1925*

Vita roused in you what Leonard did not.
Thrillingly aristocratic, a ship in full sail.

Sitting on your floor in her velvet jacket
as you knotted her pearls.

When she threatened to drive to Monk's House late,
throw gravel at your window and spend the night

you telegraphed: 'Come then'. She was what you
had never been – a *real woman*, controlling

silver, servants, chow dogs. But you saw
what was missing, that thing that didn't vibrate

at the core. The ardour you could not supply
she swiftly sought in other lovers.

The legacy of your affair:
enduring friendship; memories

of those nights
you did not write about.

Ethel

'I get, generally, two letters daily. I daresay the old fires of Sapphism are blazing for the last time.'
—*Virginia Woolf, diary, 16 June 1930*

In Vita's wake
what should land in your lap

but an elderly Sapphist
in a three-cornered hat.

A general's daughter –
lusty, loquacious,

persistent, deaf,
demanding

her hour of glory,
your attention, all the details.

Commanding an orchestra,
commanding the room.

You admired her gallantry
in the face of failure.

Found a new frankness
in missives for her eyes.

Deplored the tempestuous scenes
she thrived on.

Rose up indignant
against her jealous claims.

Basked in the blaze.

The pouch of Douglas

'Although eponyms should be avoided, they are in frequent use and a guide to their meaning is useful.'
—*O'Rahilly,* Anatomy

a friend who went for a pelvic ultrasound was relieved to hear she had no unusual fluids in her pouch of Douglas

what she didn't know was that the pouch of Douglas is a small pocket in the female body in which reside all the eponyms that physicians have tacked onto this extraordinary anatomy

filed alphabetically, and if you care to look you'll see Bartholin's glands right next to Frankenhauser's ganglion, which rubs up against the Graafian follicle

the canal of Nuck, on the other hand, will be found nestled between Mackinrodt's ligament and the tubules of Skene

so where exactly *is* this pouch of Douglas? it is in fact the little space between the back of the uterus and the front of the rectum

two good solid names that at least a woman can call her own

Making pipettes

Rolling the hollow rod above the bunsen,
blue flame glowing orange where fire embraces glass,
turning it in the fingertips watching for something
almost ineffable, the particular shine that denotes
a particular malleability.

Then taking the rod from the flame
and in one swift even motion stretching it,
six inches for a pipette (if making
capillary tubes, the full arms' length
as if to say This far! to a sceptical crowd).

If attempted prematurely, it will force a sluggish length
that cramps up again too soon;
left too late and the rod's slack belly
will droop into the fire, irreparably deviate.

Once the tube is cooled, take a file
and make a nick
at mid-point where you will snap it, rendering
two tiny mouths wide-open; fitting to the other end
a rubber bulb, a lung, to draw up some solution
that mustn't touch the skin.

Patience, narrow observation and precision are required
to forge this least precise of measures.
A certain dramatic flair merely adds to the pleasure.

| 50 |
| **Sn** |
| Tin |

I turn to pick up four empty cans,
turn to place them
on the narrow conveyor belt.

The cans are steel, plated with tin.
Pure tin, when deformed,
makes a sound – the 'tin cry'.

It will do this over and over
until it snaps. Another day,
another line. I check the code

on the top of each can.
Reject the non-conformers
and the dented, where tin's

crucial seal might be ruptured.
Three times a day
the machines grind to silence.

While others seek coffee,
sustenance, chat,
I chain smoke in the toilet.

Next year I'll implode. My life's
shiny surface breached,
revealing the old corrosion.

82
Pb
Lead

Inorganic chemistry lab. A rack of test tubes
filled with colourless solutions.

Drops of another transparent liquid added.
In each tube, something new appears:

a precipitate, an insoluble solid,
which may be crystalline, curdy, colloidal;

may float as a flocculent mass, or plummet
brightly coloured to the bottom.

I was blind to my feelings for my friend.
One drunken night recognition bloomed.

Add a drop of lead nitrate to potassium iodide:
a canary bursts forth from a clear sky.

20
Ca
Calcium

A flask is laid on the electronic scale
and tared to zero. I start with a small job lot,
topped up with smaller and smaller

increments. Index finger gently taps
the silver spatula's side, loosing a miniature
sheet of fine unseasonable snow.

In nature this white powder begins
as millions of tiny skeletons, compressed
by their own multitudinous weight

and the roaring bulk of the sea. Now it will buffer
the pH of the medium, allow me to cultivate
many crinkled circular sheets of mould.

I don't know why I'm growing mould.
I don't know what I will do with my life.
But watching and measuring I accrete

habits of precision, observation; learn
the power of purposeful repetition, the thrill
when the first portion added is exact.

11
Na
Sodium

a metal so light it floats
a metal you can cut with a knife
a metal never found free in nature

when a shaving is pared away
sodium's cut surface
shines glorious silver

but tarnishes in seconds
that incredible lustre
transformed to the dull grey of sodium oxides

heated in air, sodium burns
with a brilliant golden-yellow flame
tossed into water, it explodes

neat sodium must be swaddled
in a nonreactive substance
stored under kerosene, under oil

I wanted to be the pure metal
solely myself, self-sufficient,
swaddled in the safety

of needing no one
now I know we're never pure
beginning as we do as admixture

a dollop
of the genetically new,
from the outset, chemically intermingled

then we separate, but never completely
even when we feel entirely alone
our mirror neurons

prove us liars, firing
when we see the other damaged
or delighted, as if it were

our hand
poked with a blunt needle
or stroked by another's hand

I grew up in a house of liars
a houseful of people
pretending to be separate

but humans are never
found free in nature
it's how we're designed – connection

as vital as oxygen
intermingled, impure
we shine

Scar massage

a tiny section of my body
was excised, sent off for biopsy

a day or two later
somebody jokingly asked
how I thought my mole was going

I found I could not bear to think of
that small piece of me
floating in clear fluid in a plastic bottle
in a pathologist's office

irretrievable, irrevocably
exiled

I was left with a cavity
that has sealed itself over
with the help of two continuous sutures

now that the stitches are out and a week has gone by
I massage the scar for five minutes twice a day
using, as advised, two fingers
and as much pressure as I can tolerate
to prevent the join
hardening

I am astounded by the depth of its colour

other parts of me have been lost
other scars left to harden

these are not so visible

I have stopped ignoring them nonetheless
have stopped trying to disguise them
with complaisance, competence, facts-at-the-ready

I return to them, feel for
their shapes under the surface
attest their presence
with as much pressure as I can tolerate

I speak to them

tell them
that they are no longer alone

Everything including the obvious

for Cynthia

how can I describe you, my surprise, my unpredictable
your mind encompasses multitudes while I
am down on my knees squinting at the particular

your brain works sideways like a crab but in every direction at once
    on many levels
no point asking what you're thinking – too many things to list
though sometimes I ask you to toss me three at random

the tips of all ideas have handles, their wholenesses dangling below
you flash the handles and I learn to catch them

for the sake of internal peace you're learning to winnow
but your taste for multiplicity expands me,
flavours our life together, my habit of discernment a seasoning

by comparison I'm a slow simplistic one-track wonder
gathering towards potential actions in my steadfast cumulative
    felt-sensed way

shake it up! you say
willing to lose it all to gain it all
in your world everything including the obvious

just one of the possibilities

Notes

8   The changes
In bell-ringing, 'ringing the changes' means ringing a tuned set of bells in a series of patterns. Each pattern is called a change.

9   Come in, lie down
'I must go down to the seas again' is the opening line of John Masefield's poem 'Sea-Fever'.

16   Nessa
Vanessa Bell (née Stephen) was Virginia Woolf's older sister. The phrase 'dry and dusty' is from a letter from Woolf to Bell, 2 October 1937.

17   Vita
Vita is Vita Sackville-West. Virginia's affair with Vita was at its peak in the years 1925–28. Leonard is Leonard Woolf, who Virginia married in 1912. The phrases 'real woman', 'silver, servants, chow dogs' are from Virginia Woolf's diary, 21 December 1925.

18   Ethel
Dame Ethel Smyth was a British composer, conductor and author, and a prominent activist for women's suffrage.

Acknowledgements

'Making pipettes' appeared in *Law and Impulse* (Science Made Marvellous anthology, Brook Emery, Victoria Haritos and Carol Jenkins, eds, Poets Union, 2010) and was an Australian National Science Week 2013 Science Poem of the Day. It also appeared in Tricia Dearborn's collection *Frankenstein's Bathtub* (Interactive Press: Emerging Poets Series, 2001), as did 'The white dress' and 'The pouch of Douglas'.

'She reconsiders life on the run' appeared in *Out of the Box: Contemporary Australian Gay and Lesbian Poets* (Michael Farrell and Jill Jones, eds, Puncher & Wattmann, 2010); 'The changes' appeared in *Australian Poetry since 1788* (Geoffrey Lehmann and Robert Gray, eds, UNSW Press, 2011) and *Notes to the Translators* (Kit Kelen, ed., ASM Poetry, 2012); 'Come in, lie down' appeared in *Southerly* (2007), *The Best Australian Poetry 2008* (David Brooks, ed., UQP), *Australian Poetry since 1788* and on *Poetica*, ABC Radio National, 'Round the Nation' (2013). All of these poems also appeared in Tricia Dearborn's collection *The Ringing World* (Puncher & Wattmann, 2012), as did 'The smiley spoon' and 'The quiet house'.

'Sanctuary' appeared in *Marrickville Pause* (2018); 'Phlegm: a love poem' appeared in *Cordite Poetry Review* (2017); 'Tin' and 'Lead' appeared in *Island Magazine* (2018); '[20] Calcium' appeared in *Cordite Poetry Review* (2017); '[11] Sodium' appeared in *The Best Australian Science Writing 2019* (Bianca Nogrady, ed., NewSouth); 'Scar massage' appeared in *Not Very Quiet* (2018) and *Australian Poetry Anthology* (Yvette Holt and Magan Magan, eds, 2019); 'Everything including the obvious' appeared in *Cordite Poetry Review* (2018). All of these poems also appeared in Tricia Dearborn's collection *Autobiochemistry* (UWAP, 2019), as did 'A chalk outline of the soul', 'Nessa', 'Vita' and 'Ethel'.

Tricia Dearborn is an award-winning poet whose work has been widely published in Australian literary journals, as well as in the UK, the US, Ireland, New Zealand and online. Her poetry is well-represented in significant anthologies including *Contemporary Australian Poetry* and *Australian Poetry since 1788*. She is on the editorial board of *Plumwood Mountain*, an online journal of ecopoetry and ecopoetics, and was a judge for the inaugural Quantum Words Science Poetry Competition in 2018. She has received a number of grants from the Australia Council, and has been awarded two residencies at Varuna, the Writers' House. Her published collections are *The Ringing World*, *Frankenstein's Bathtub*, and *Autobiochemistry* (UWA Publishing, 2019).

IPSI: International Poetry Studies Institute

The International Poetry Studies Institute (IPSI) is part of the Centre for Creative and Cultural Research, Faculty of Arts and Design, University of Canberra. IPSI conducts research related to poetry, and publishes and promulgates the outcomes of this research internationally. The institute also publishes poetry and interviews with poets, as well as related material, from around the world. Publication of such material takes place in IPSI's online journal *Axon: Creative Explorations* (www.axonjournal.com.au). IPSI's goals include working – collaboratively, where possible – for the appreciation and understanding of poetry, poetic language and the cultural and social significance of poetry. The institute also organises symposia, seminars, readings and other poetry-related activities and events.

IPSI Chapbook Series

The IPSI Chapbook Series publishes new work by leading poets from Australia and beyond. The chapbooks feature extended selections beyond the scope of most journals, highlighting innovative work by poets both new and established. The series is linked to an international program of poets in residence at the University of Canberra.

Series Editor: Paul Munden.

CCCR: Centre for Creative and Cultural Research

The Centre for Creative and Cultural Research (CCCR) is IPSI's umbrella organisation and brings together staff, adjuncts, research students and visiting fellows who work on key challenges within the cultural sector and creative field. A central feature of its research concerns the effects of digitisation and globalisation on cultural producers, whether individuals, communities or organisations.

www.ingramcontent.com/pod-product-compliance
Ingram Content Group UK Ltd.
Pitfield, Milton Keynes, MK11 3LW, UK
UKHW021323180426
11947UKWH00017B/1410